QUOTES FOR THE MENTALITY NOTES FOR THE REALITY

ANTONIA HARRIS

Kravitz & Sons
INNOVATORS IN PUBLISHING, MARKETING AND ADVERTISING

Kravitz and Sons LLC
1301 Farmville Blvd, Suite 104
Greenville, NC 27834

Published by Kravitz and Sons LLC.
ISBN: 979-8-89639-502-7 (sc)
ISBN: 979-8-89639-503-4 (e)

Library of Congress Control Number: 2025917476

To the world, with love and care

Quote for Today

Day 1

Conditions

There are people in life who deal with a disease, like arthritis, influenza, asthma, lupus, cancer, and people who are diabetics…

Some people that deal with the disease do not do what they got to do to survive, no excuse, it does make it pathetic…

Some people that deal with the disease do what they got to do, respectfully, to avoid complications, without any static…

No matter what, either way of the feeling and dealing, stay prayed up; this would be highly recommended and so fantastic…

There are many other people dealing with other types of diseases, which is included in the theory, Staying Prayed Up, avoid the drastic…

Always take care of yourself, self comes first, follow directions, take precautions, have self-control, take care of your health, automatic…

Stay prayed up…

Quote for Today

Day 2

Known Factors

Sometimes people take information and twist it so it seems like it is a known factor…

Sometimes people take information and get it twisted, which that part could matter…

Sometimes when people twist what was known as a factor, in ways of being naive…

Sometimes when people get it twisted, and it matters, no one wants to believe…

Stay prayed up…

Quote for Today

Day 3

The Meaning of *Positive*

P—Proud—making moments to achieve...

O—Outstanding—accomplishments that you receive...

S—Satisfy—a feeling to be relieved...

I—Intelligent—a done dance when conceived...

T—Talent—your trick up your own sleeve...

I—Innocent—it is the truth to believe...

V—Victory—confidence that you will succeed...

E—Energy—depends on mind, body, and soul, like Adam and Eve...

Stay prayed up...

Quote for Today

Day 4

The Meaning of *Negative*

N—Naughty—not nice, rather be rude than cool…

E—Evil—do things on purpose acting a fool…

G—Grudge—held tight, upright like a heavy tool…

A—Attitude—been there done that, just like in high school…

T—Tuff—not scared, will point you out, like it's you'll…

I—Intimidate—to put down, like a torn piece of wool…

V—Vicious—not stopping, out of control like drowning in a pool…

E—Erupted—over the limit, no brakes to pump, which is not Kool…

Stay prayed up…

Quote for Today

Day 5

Like It or Not

Sometimes people don't like other people for absolutely no reason at all, you lose points, and why when it could be possible, you get edited…

Sometimes people do like other people crudely although pleasing at fall, you gain anoints, and try when it should be solvable, you get credited…

This would go either way, the don't like or like, continue to stay prayed up, either way could be dreaded and spreaded…

Stay prayed up…

Quote for Today

Day 6

Agenda Hidden

Sometimes it is best to keep your secrets, a secret, meaning be careful who you open up to, because some people want a testimony, and some people want tea…

Sometimes it is stress to keep your infrequents, a infrequent, meaning be forgetful due you open up to because some people front a ceremony and, some people front flee.

Sometimes it is test to keep your delinquents, a delinquent, meaning be declareful do you open up to because some people want a prestimony, and some people stunt thee…

Sometimes it is bless to keep your frequents, a frequent, meaning be spiritful to whom you open up to because some people blunt a alimony, and some people blunt free…

The point is secret, infrequent, delinquent, and frequent, indicates something within you; just remember, you are in with the something…

The moral is testimony, ceremony, prestimony, and alimony indicate nothing therein you; just remember, you are in there the nothing…

Stay prayed up…

Quote for Today

Day 7

Greatness

The feeling of love…

The feeling above…

The wonderful lives of the creation…

The thankful strives of the nation…

The words of wisdom we must say…

The overall power we must pray…

The faith, the belief is more, it is not less…

The moral is God is great, we are blessed…

Stay prayed up…

Quote for Today

Day 8

Mindset

Sometimes the mind have people sense different things…

(If it is a bad thing, no, if it is a good thing, change…)

Sometimes the heart have people feel some type of way…

(If it is a bad feel, no, if it is a good feel, pray…)

Sometimes the mind and heart could be held with tightness…

Regardless how the mind and heart could be held, let it be filled with brightness…

Stay prayed up…

Quote for Today

Day 9

The Company

Some people are evil, where they try to tear you down...

Some people are caring, those are the ones to be around...

Some people will wish you no good luck, when your back is turnt, they frown...

Some people will wish you best luck, now would you rather hear that sound...

Sometimes people may not know who wishes the no luck or best of luck, and that is the plan...

Sometimes it could be the devil walking through, which is not the man, but you must continue to stand...

Stay prayed up...

Quote for Today

Day 10

The Verified

Sometimes when people show their guide, it could indicate actual length...

Sometimes when people glow their pride, it would indicate factual strength...

Sometimes when people know their survive, it should indicate casual tenth...

The point is, guide, pride, and survive is very natural and should come naturally as a caring person...

The moral is length, strength, and tenth is very collateral and could some collaterally as a sharing certain...

Stay prayed up...

Quote for Today

Day 11

It Takes Two

There are two types of being tired; the tired that requires rest, and the tired that requires peace...

There are two types of being admired; the admired that acquires guest, and the admired that acquires release...

There are two types of being desired; the desired that transpires suggest, and the desired that transpires surcease...

There are two types of being inspired; the inspired that desires best, and the inspired that desires increase...

The point is *tired*, *admired*, *desired*, and *inspired* are words that are connected, and wired, but can be used separately...

The moral is *peace*, *release*, *surcease*, and *increase* are words that are neglected, and expired, but can be profused desperately...

Stay prayed up...

Quote for Today

Day 12

Learning Experience

Sometimes people learn different things from other people, and what is learned should always be good...

Sometimes people copy off of other people, which is irrelevant but was never understood...

Sometimes the people who did learn something, is proud of what they was taught...

Sometimes the people who do copy something, eventually do get caught...

Learn and copy is all up to you, the point is what would be God's thought...

Stay prayed up...

Quote for Today

Day 13

The Seesaw

Sometimes things and situations could be a challenge...

Sometimes it could be rough or smooth, just keep your balance...

Sometimes the thing or situation could be unpredicted and wrong...

No matter if that is the case, make a sacrifice, and do not prolong...

Sometimes the thing or situation could be predicted, and right...

No matter if that is the case, continue on that journey and shine bright...

Stay prayed up...

Quote for Today

Day 14

Giving

Sometimes people give off energy that may be iffy because they play both sides…

Sometimes people give off energy that could be admired, respecting your pride…

Sometimes people that are the interaction, stirring wrong and wants people to collide…

Sometimes people that are outside of the intersection, energy tight, which would you decide…

Stay prayed up…

Quote for Today

Day 15

Face Card

Sometimes it comes to a point, that people are two-faced...:

"Two-faced is hypocritical"

Sometimes it comes to a point, that people become erased...

"Erased is critical"

Sometimes it comes to a point, people want too much space...

"Space is interval"

Sometimes it comes to a point, where two-faced, erased, and space should be disconnected...

The summary of these points is to use the terms wisely and always stay connected...

Stay prayed up...

Quote for Today

Day 16

Hold On

Some people know how to hold their own and stand on their own two feet, being a dedicated person…

Some people depend on others, always got their hands out, which is below standards but their version…

Some people know how to maintain without asking people for nothing…

Some people do get the concept and always asking people for something…

Some people may feel to give up but jump right back to their normal ego…

Some people feel not to give up but then do something that is illegal…

Stay prayed up…

Quote for Today

Day 17

Have No Fear

Sometimes the people that have guilt, pretend, because they have no fear...

Sometimes the people that are innocent, amend, because they were far, now near...

Sometimes when people are guilty, they play victim to aim and win...

Sometimes when people are innocent, their dignity is looked at as a sin...

Sometimes when people are guilty, they do not own up to their own parade...

Sometimes when people are innocent, their spirits are shown as being portrayed...

Stay prayed up...

Quote for Today

Day 18

Loyalty

Sometimes the people who are loyal, usually stay loyal, because they are unique and have specialized hearts…

Sometimes the people who are unloyal, stay unloyal, because towards you, they are being smart…

Sometimes when loyal people come to a freeze, is it that they are being real and true…

Sometimes when unloyal people dumb to they tease, it is that they disbar seeing ordeal or clue…

Sometimes loyal people have that sensation, they ride and vibe, and they know who they are…

Sometimes unloyal people be cocky, shy but why, they are the ones to stay away from and disregard…

Stay prayed up…

Quote for Today

Day 19

Straight Line

Sometimes people get out of line, which could be a challenge…

Sometimes people stay in line, which would be a talent…

Getting out of line could go way too far, or to an extreme extent…

Staying in line should be for the best, stay prayed up, and do not repent…

Stay prayed up…

Quote for Today

Day 20

Humor

Sometimes people's sense of humor is bland, and they don't know how to interact...

Sometimes people's sense of humor is glad, and they most likely do attract...

Sometimes people do not know how to let out their expressions, because they are shy...

Sometimes people who show their expressions is a go, and you do not have to question why...

Stay prayed up...

Quote for Today

Day 21

Determination

Sometimes people make decisions, when it comes to relationships, that they are only there to mingle...

Sometimes people make visions, when it comes to relationships, make it known that they are not single...

Sometimes the mingle thing can lead to confusion and turn into a mess...

Sometimes the people who are not single lead to their conclusion, to say less...

The people who decide to mingle sometimes bring something to the table that you may have to reconsider...

The people who are not single sometimes bring their commitment and be stable, a big compliment that they have no filter...

Stay prayed up...

Quote for Today

Day 22

Bridges

Sometimes people burn their bridges, which is okay to them, but what about the person you burned…

Sometimes people do not burn their bridges, which is okay to them, and this would be more firm…

Sometimes the people who are burned or burned you, may need a favor or something down the line…

Sometimes the people who do not burn their bridges are considerate, which is fair and fine…

The moral is watch who you burn bridges with cause them same people you can need…

On another note, the people who respect their limits and bridges, stay prayed up, now that is the lead…

Stay prayed up…

Quote for Today

Day 23

Heartless

Let your heart beat slow, nice, quiet, and tender…

Let your mind think wisely, good things to remember…

When your heart beats it alerts, if your heart is in the right place…

When you think your mind should always alert you, to keep a smile on your face…

Even if your heart starts to pound, keep your spirit high. And do not let it sink…

Even if your mind begins to feel overwhelmed, stay prayed up, that is what to think…

Stay prayed up…

Quote for Today

Day 24

Relations

Sometimes people have a relationship with you (anything pertaining to a connection) but do not take it as mutual…

Sometimes people have a relationship with you (anything pertaining to a connection) and know how to connect like usual…

Sometimes when people do connect, are not the right people that should be connected…

Sometimes when people do not connect, are the right people, it is the vibe that's respected…

Watch the people who you be around…

Some could be actin'…

Watch the people who hold the connection down…

The real ones do not be slacken…

Stay prayed up…

Quote for Today

Day 25

Reality

Life is precious, life is short, make every moment matter, and make it your best...

Life could be hard, life could be a struggle, but sometimes life will put you through a test...

Life could be deadly, life could be taken, live life we do not know our time to nest...

Life could be fun, life is what you make it, but staying prayed up is the important request...

Stay prayed up...

Antonia's Quote for Today

Day 26

Life

My quotes for today represents awareness, life, nothing personal that I'm going through, it is called reality and inspiration...

My notes are to encourage, give examples, life, giving back with some knowledge and clues, it is called mentality and preparation...

Stay prayed up...

Quote for Today

Day 27

Level Up

When people anticipate to try to manipulate your brain with negativity, block it with your frontal lobe, and remember it is science, but more important, it is all about your compliance...

When people participate to try to initiate your pain with toxicity, lock it with your prefrontal probe, and remember it is alliance, but more important, it is all about your defiance...

When people liberate to try to discriminate your gain with hostility, knock it with your subtle code and remember it is subsidence, but more important, it is all about your reliance...

When people eliminate to try to deliberate your maintain with conductivity, rock it with your rebuttal abode, and remember it is contrivance, but more important, it is all about your guidance...

Stay prayed up...

Quote for Today

Day 28

Colors

Roses are red, Violets are blue

We cannot predict the future; we have no clue...

Bananas are yellow, trees are green

Tomorrow is not promised, staying prayed up and clean...

Birds do chirp, dogs do bark...

This would be a part of nature, but our living must be worth your while, and not wild but sharp...

This should be on the chart...

Stay prayed up...

Quote for Today

Day 29

Seasons

There are four seasons in a year, not equally divided by the months, it is when they appear…

When the four seasons approach on their times, not sequently sided it cannot be compared….

Spring, the weather turns warm, it is lite and delicate, where seeds take root, and vegetation begins to grow…

Summer, the weather turns hot, it is short, it is after spring, but autumn foreshadows, and it is a bright glow…

Fall is autumn, which is blustery, breezy, and slight, when the certain colors are worn, then you will know…

Winter is colder weather, snow, frost, and ice, some may like it, some may not like it, this one is between a so-so…

The four seasons may not be simple and basic for some when they do arrive…

Know how to deal with temperature change and dressing accordingly, your way to survive…

Stay prayed up…

Quote for Today

Day 30

Requirements

The amount of water required: woman 11.5 cups (2.7 liters), men 15.5 cups (3.7 liters), this is a good technique to stay hydrated...

The types of foods to choose should exclude what is bad for you, some like beef and pork, and yes that part should always stay updated...

The point is when deciding what water to drink, and the types of food to eat, know the amount, make healthier choices, and stay involved...

Doing research, getting advice, trying it out can be beneficial to your health, either you regret it, or it can pay and be resolved...

Healthy choices to a better lifestyle...

Stay prayed up...

Quote for Today

Day 31

Picture Perfect

Sometimes people will point a pretty picture, but that picture they painted, does not mean that they are an artist...

Sometimes people will draw you in close, because you are their enemy, and keeping you close would be the smartest...

Sometimes the people that paint that pretty picture and draw you in close, they could be sneaky and known as a narcissist...

Sometimes people will paint an ugly picture, but that picture that they painted was painted to be seen, and not undercover...

Sometimes the people that draw you in close, because they have a different approach, nothing to hide, and nothing to discover...

The moral is watch the way people paint and draw, admire well and prevent, the choice they make could be iffy and blow their cover...

Stay prayed up...

Quote for Today

Day 32

Flashing Lights

The color of the traffic lights are red, yellow, and green, it could be helpful using these colors, it could be beneficial to reach your dreams...

Red could indicate that you are not in the right lane, and that you must stay in between the lines, and try turning on your high beams...

Yellow could indicate that sometimes you have to break, but when it is time to merge, stay to the right, that direction is the mainstreams...

Green could indicate to Go, keep it moving, and drive your proper speed, but know your speed limit, and know when to go and wow that seems...

Stay prayed up...

Quote for Today

Day 33

Dictation

Sometimes when people speculate, it is based off their insecurities, and to guess is their desire, which is their own intuition, on how they construct passion...

Sometimes when people regulate, it is based off their theories, and their test is their empire, which is their condition, on how to conduct their type of compassion...

Sometimes when people bate, it is based off their immaturity, and there is no rest, then their reflection conspires, which is their mission, on how to destruct and imagine...

Sometimes when people create, it is based off their purities, not no mess, their actions inspires, which is their prediction, it is their normal instruct, a valid transaction...

Stay prayed up...

Quote for Today

Day 34

Leadership

Sometimes people will follow the leader, the leader could be conniving and deceiving, and to hold that spot, they will not apologize…

Sometimes people will follow the leader, the leader could be achieving and succeeding, and to withhold that pot, honorly to legalize…

Sometimes the leader will have followers, that follower could be the wrong candidate, which could get tacky and livid…

Sometimes the leader will have followers, the follower could be right to validate, which would be more fitted…

The point is that actual leaders shows what really needs to be done, their lead is all about perfection…

The moral is the natural followers knows what they really needs to be fun, their lead is all about selection…

Stay prayed up…

Quote for Today

Day 35

Situations

Sometimes people are subliminal to what they are told, it may seem legit, but could be mendacious about the tale, which could be taken as authentic without proof...

Sometimes people are liminal to what they behold, it is redeemed credit, but would be audacious about the mail, which should be taken as magnetic with the truth...

Sometimes people do not dare, to elaborate their translation property, the slur could indicate what is being spoken, and it could appear shameful...

Sometimes people do be fair, to deliberate their information nontoxicity, the blur would initiate what is being broken, and it would stare tameful...

Stay prayed up...

Quote for Today

Day 36

Benefit of the Doubt

Sometimes when you give people the benefit of the doubt, they will proceed to underestimate you until you have maxed out...

Sometimes when you give people the fundament of the drought, they will exceed to eliminate you, not knowing what's it about...

Sometimes when people take precaution, their integrity becomes inflated, which reflects on their type of betterment...

Sometimes when people choose their option, their clarity becomes populated, which detects on their type of commitment...

Stay prayed up...

Quote for Today

Day 37

Willpower

Sometimes when people analyze their own expectations, and what they expect could be a flash, depending, but it is not about their way, it is about their will...

Sometimes when people fantasize their own demonstrations, and what they demonstrate could be a clash, pending, but it is not about their play, it is about their ordeal...

Sometimes when people tantalize their own exclamations, and what they exclaim could be a pass, ending, but it is not about the say, it is about their chill...

Sometimes when people classify their own negotiations, and what they negotiate could be a blast, tending, but it is not about their okay, it is about their skill...

Sometimes when people dramatize their own hallucinations, and what they hallucinate could be a lash, offending, but it is not about their display, it is about their thrill...

The point is when you deal with "-ize," it could indicate whatever, but be clever, treat it or handle it, like milk "pasteurized" and get rid of it…

The moral is when you deal with "-ing," it could mandate forever, but be better, beat it or cancel it, like ilk "sterilized," and the lid should fit…

Stay prayed up…

Quote for Today

Day 38

Clown

Sometimes people are actors, which could represent to be oblivious, but their act could be a bystander...

Sometimes people are slackers, which could decent to be hideous, but their slack could be a handler...

Sometimes people are detractors, which could prevent to be invidious, but their detract could be a manner...

Sometimes people are factors, which could consent to be piteous, but their fact could be a standard...

Stay prayed up...

Quote for Today

Day 39

Be Aware

Sometimes the "walk" of a person could indicate their approach, which could be mysterious, but that is their way to make it clear…

Sometimes the "talk" of a person could indicate their encroach, which could be serious, but their play to create fit care…

Sometimes the "gawk" of a person could indicate their coach, which could be delirious, but their delay to fake bit fear…

Sometimes the "stalk" of a person could indicate their gauche, which could be supercilious, but their say to sake hit rare…

Stay prayed up…

Quote for Today

Day 40

Characteristics

Sometimes people character could indicate the type of baggage there to be attended, which it cannot be the same as boutique...

Sometimes people character could indicate the type of savage there to be offended, which cannot be like claim as unique...

Sometimes people character could indicate the type of package there to be suspended, which it cannot be the blame as critique...

Sometimes people character could indicate the type of trackage there to be pretended, which it cannot be the game as technique...

Stay prayed up...

Quote for Today

Day 41

Truth Be Told

Sometimes people deliver information that tries to be anachronistic, showing integrity, stimulating factual, but the message is rancorous...

Sometimes people quiver dictation that lies to be mystic, flowing prosperity, cumulating actual, but the wreckage is magnanimous...

Sometimes people shiver formation that denies the altruistic, blowing sincerity, articulating natural, but the presage is languorous...

Sometimes people stiver vexation that replies the dyslogistic, knowing disparity, scintillating casual, but the coverage is rapturous...

Stay prayed up...

Quote for Today

Day 42

Guard Up

Sometimes people's distractions, on the meaning of shield, could be protection, reflection, which could indicate an unknown speculation of ostentatious…

Sometimes people's attractions, on the leaning of build, could be selection, connection, which could initiate the obvious allegation of flirtatious…

Sometimes people's reactions, on the cleaning of wield, could be collection, detection, which could propitiate an unblown hesitation of predacious…

Sometimes people's detractions, on the demeaning of yield, could be objection, direction, which could humiliate the odious preparation of fallacious…

Stay prayed up…

Quote for Today

Day 43

Real Talk

Sometimes for some people when their reality sets in, sike tension of a hard base...

Sometimes for some people when their mentality sets in, like detention of a barred case...

The base of reality is stronger, wiser, smarter, and really knowing about their reality...

The case of mentality is wronger, riser, farther, and really showing about their mentality...

Some people may take reality as a game, playing around, and as a simple joke...

Some people may create mentality as a shame, staying down, and pass a nimble vote...

The point is however the case, base, reality, and your mentality, or the jokes and votes may be perceived...

The moral is forever the grace, embrace, totality, and your practicality, of the notes and quotes may be conceived...

Stay prayed up...

Quote for Today

Day 44

Only You

No one has walked in another person's shoes, because we all are one of a kind…

No one can tell another person's story, because we all have our own minds…

No one could be exactly like another person, because we are built from different designs…

No one has talked in another person's clues, because we all are one of uncombined…

No one can feel another person's glory, because we all have our thrown inclined…

No one could be actually like another person, because we are rebuilt from different opined…

Only you know you, and can't nobody tell you about you…

Only you glow through, and can't nobody well you about through…

The point is to be kind, have a clear mind, and continue to use pretty designs…

The moral is free uncombined, have a dear inclined, and continue to amuse signs…

Stay prayed up…

Quote for Today

Day 45

Indirect

Sometimes when people speak, they speak indirectly...

Sometimes when people look, they look incorrectly...

Sometimes when people touch, they touch disrespectfully...

Sometimes when people sneak, they sneak ineptly...

Sometimes when people shook, they shock hypercorrectly...

Sometimes when people clutch, they clutch intently...

Speaking, looking, and touching is known to be part of our senses...

When indirectly, incorrectly, and disrespectfully is known to bring tension...

Sneaking, shooking, and clutching is prone to depart of our pretenses...

When ineptly, hypercorrectly, and intently is shown to bring dissension...

The point is when the word described ends in -ly, just fade it all out…

The moral is when the word subscribed ends in -ion, must trade it fall doubt…

Stay prayed up…

Quote for Today

Day 46

Remember

Remember, as you should understand more and more that it is not about what you look like or what you own, it is about the person you have become...

Remember, as you could demand for and for that it is spot about what you took sike or what you shown, it is about the immersion you have overcome...

Remember, as you would command before and before that it is forgot about what you rook unlike or what you unknown, it is about the reassertion you have from...

Remember, as you good expand adore and adore that it is hot about what you shook dislike or what you thrown, it is about you have some...

Stay prayed up...

Quote for Today

Day 47

The Gym

Sometimes when people want to gain and strengthen, they make up stories to make them look good, which is not the way to hold weight…

Sometimes when people want to maintain and lengthen, they take up inventories to take them hook stood, which is slot the play to mold straight…

Sometimes when people want to train and extension, they make up explories to make them crook wood, which is forgot the say to bold pernitrate…

Sometimes when people want to remain and tendon, they take up glories to take them took understood, which is hot the pray to sold update…

Stay prayed up…

Quote for Today

Day 48

Strength

Sometimes when people's acumen becomes cynosure, it could indicate their mold of weakness, but what is the predilection...

Sometimes when people's human becomes composure, it could insinuate their scold of sneakiness, but what is the intellection...

Sometimes when people's obtuseness - becomes overexposure, it could dictate their fold of leakiness, but what is the injection...

Sometimes when people's pompousness becomes enclosure, it could vindicate their hold of peakness, but what is the question...

Stay prayed up...

Quote for Today

Day 49

Gut Feeling

Sometimes when people's conscious is second-guessed, it underlines the thoughts, and intuition going on in their gut...

Sometimes when people's semiconscious is reckoned lessed, it defines the naughts, and recognition going on in their hut...

Sometimes when people's subconscious is beckoned expressed, it declines the foughts, and disposition going on in their stunt...

Sometimes people's nonconscious is checkoned impressed, it combines the taughts and demolition going on in their shut...

Stay prayed up...

Quote for Today

Day 50

Actuality

Sometimes people are set to be convivial, which may indicate their indication of dystychiphobia, but the topic reveals twisted metanoia...

Sometimes people are far bet to be trivial, which play mediate their mediation of toxicophobia, but the logic ideals desisted paranoia...

Sometimes people star let to be critical, which say depreciate their depreciation of cornucopia, but the chronic conceals insisted hyponoia...

Sometimes people scar forget to be jovial, which pray remediate their remediation of anhedonia, but sardonic appeals unlisted gloss phobia...

Stay prayed up...

Quote for Today

Day 51

The Sequence

Sometimes when people's thoughts are candor, it could bring something rank to your table...

Sometimes when people's taughts are pander, it could sting something prank to your able...

Sometimes when people's foughts are slander, it could ring something crank to your stable...

Sometimes when people's caughts are standard, it could cling something stank to your label...

Stay prayed up...

Quote for Today

Day 52

Basic

Sometimes when people change or act different, it could mean, truck it, pluck it, or two tears in a bucket, and at the end, it is considered their own loss...

Sometimes when people rearrange or fact munificent, it should clean, luck it, tuck it, or few clears in a duck it, and at the send, it is delivered their own cost...

The point is when the individual is proving, it is a stick or wrap, use your intelligence wisely and just do you...

The moral is when the original is moving, it is a tic or tac abstruse your evidence concisely and dust to who...

Stay prayed up...

Quote for Today

Day 53

Bank It

Sometimes when people take a withdrawal, it could validate, their checking could bounce…

Sometimes when people make a deposit, it should obliterate, their savings should amount…

Sometimes when people are negative, their mentality is transferred to ounce…

Sometimes when people are positive, their reality is preferred to surmount…

The point is, if you allow people to make more withdrawals than deposits in your life, you will be out of balance and negative, know when to close your account…

The moral is, if you vow people to take score noncausals than profits in your despite, you will be out of allowance and in the positive, below when to froze your discount…

When you use your mentality, always think which bank you should choose, because some of the tellers is out to make you lose money...

When you profuse your reality, always think which rank you should moose, because some of the sellers is about to take you misuse honey...

Stay prayed up...

Quote for today

Day 54

Brainstorm

Sometimes when the brain is underlined by your mind, it could indicate that the thoughts are filtered, which could seem right, but actually is wrong...

Sometimes when the pain is defined by your blind, it would initiate that the foughts are litered, which would deem bright, but habitually is strong...

Sometimes when the gains is combined by your kind, it should anticipate that the aughts are splintered, which should gleam light, but factually is belong...

Stay prayed up...

Quote for Today

Day 55

UNO

Let's not withdrawal a clue, why obsolete what was already none, no game, but it is trade doubt, maybe a little game…

Do not change the wild color, that selection is the experience of wanting better, slow pace, one step only and claim…

Do not rearrange the mild other, that perfection is the incipience of wanting, however, glow face, redone prepped only and tame…

Let's not dwell on the wild draw four, remember at fault has turned to default. Keep striving, the point is to strive…

Let's not tell on the style fall before, September at halt has burned to exalt, steep surviving, the moral is to have survived…

The statement that is being delivered, let's not move backwards, things happen in life, the mentality of what was, no…

The embracement that is being considered, do not prove forwards, flings happen in life, the reality of what does, UNO…

Stay prayed up…

Quote for Today

Day 56

The Feel

Sometimes when people's temperature is taken, their body starts to fluctuate, which would indicate an abnormal level of the peak...

Sometimes when people's spot is shaken, their parts to insinuate, which can eliminate a normal level of the weak...

Sometimes when people's cold is waken, their darts to continuate, which plan accentuate a formal level of sneak...

Sometimes when people's hot is maken, their charts to extenuate, which began situate an informal level of streak...

Sometimes when people's scold is faken, their smarts to alternate, which scan marinate a paranormal level of leak...

Sometimes when people's expenditure is baken, their embody restarts to antagonate, which could evaluate a supernormal level of creak...

The point is, always watch your levels, they may be below, they may be above, but avoid the stress…

The moral is, always watch your settles, they say be glow, they say be love, but enjoy the bless…

Stay prayed up…

Quote for Today

Day 57

Debate

Sometimes people will have an debatement, which could lead to tinderbox, not mutual, but their obeyance is as if it is propriety...

Sometimes people still have an statement, which would plead who flummox, plot crucial, but their obeisance is as if it is the entirety...

Sometimes people chill have an placement, which could dread do faux, spot feudal, but their complaisance is as if it is the dubiety...

Sometimes people nil have an amazement, which could read boo paradox, forgot mercurial, but their allegiance is as if it is the notoriety...

Stay prayed up...

Quote for Today
Day 58

Assuming

Do not assume about a situation, when you don't know the facts...

Do not resume about an elimination, when you don't know the impacts...

Do not presume about a communication, when you don't know the exacts...

Do not consume about an information, when you don't know the acts...

Stay prayed up...

Quote for Today
Day 59

Mistake

Sometimes when the mistakes are high, they are repeated, which could mean was it really a mistake...

Sometimes when the makes are tied, they are defeated, which would mean was it really a make...

Sometimes when the forsakes are sigh, they are cheated, which should mean was it really a forsake...

Sometimes when the partakes are dried, they are beaten, which could mean was it really a partake...

Stay prayed up...

Quote for Today
Day 60

The Universe

Sometimes people may misunderstand the clear view, which could stay blocked, and not realize to feel the pinch or the tingle...

Sometimes people play band the dear crew, which should say kick rocks, stand like paralyze to heel the finch more of atingle...

Sometimes people say command the fear screw, which would stay in shocked, and plan plot apologize to steel the clinch and do mingle...

Sometimes people slay brand the bear stew, which would clay in docked, and strand rot normalize to peel the inch let be single...

Stay prayed up...

Quote for Today
Day 61

The Checklist

Sometimes people will check on you to see if you failed, and they are being nosy. Just remember, it is not about failing or what they are checking; it's about you winning…

Sometimes people spill wreck on you to see if you prevailed, and they are being cozy. Just remember, it is not about prevailing or what they are wrecking; it's about you grinning…

Sometimes people still heck on you to see if you nailed, and they are being virtuosi. Just remember, it is not about nailing or what they are hecking; it's about you beginning…

The point is failing, prevailing, and nailing all depends on you, the person, which means you have control over it all. Just remember, do not let people interfere with what you got going on, no matter how you look at it…

The moral is winning, grinning, and beginning, all intends on who, the person, which leans who have the soul over it all. Just remember, do not let people volunteer with what who got going on, no shatter how who shook at it…

Stay prayed up…

Quote for Today

Day 62

Sometiming

Sometimes people's ways, say's are considered unstable, which could mean otherwise, but their meaning is confusing...

Sometimes people's stays, delay's are reconsidered capable, which would mean surprise, but their leaning is refusing...

Sometimes people's plays, day's are bitter shapable, which should mean arise, but their intervening is losing...

Sometimes people's sways, pay's are critter shakable, which good mean disguise, but their betweening is defusing...

The point is, there are crays who think they are abusing, summarized by, the moral is, their prays do sink they are amusing...

Stay prayed up...

Quote for Today

Day 63

A Tight Edge

There are some people who have a torn heart, a broken heart, and a golden heart; make sure you pay attention to the vibes, because your heartbeat matters. Just remember, it is all about the beats...

There are some people who have a worn smart, and a token smart; make sure you pay condescension to the bribes, because your smart completely shatters. Just remember, it is all about the completes...

There are some people who have a sworn part, a spoken part, and a golden part; make sure you pay hypertension to the describes, because your part deletes scatters. Just remember, it is all about the deletes...

There are some people who have a born start, a woken start, and a bolden start; make sure you pay dimension to the subscribes because your start sweet flatters. Just remember, it is all about the sweets...

Stay prayed up...

Quote for Today

Day 64

Do Not Stress

Sometimes when people give advice, that person might need to use what they are giving to the next...

Sometimes when people give precise, that desertion tight need to confuse what they are giving to the perplexed...

Sometimes when people give nice, that assertion despite need to excuse what they are giving to the vexed...

Sometimes when people give twice, that insertion fight need to diffuse what they are giving to the text...

Stay prayed up...

Quote for Today

Day 65

The Note

Sometimes people gloat in the meaning, scary, which could ball down to "not right," but their confidence ensures their snobbery...

Sometimes when people coat in the meaning, wary, which would fall down to "plot might," but their incompetent adores their camaraderie...

Sometimes when people float in the meaning, contrary, which should appall to "spotlight," but their oscitant allures their pettifoggery...

Sometimes people bloat in the meaning, nary, which could stall down to "rot tight," but their prominence demure their bizarrerie...

Stay prayed up...

Quote for Today

Day 66

The Chapter

Sometimes people have to turn their page, because every test in life, either makes you bitter or better, and the problems that comes, with it, either break you, or make you; just remember, it is your choice, either to become victim or victory…

Sometimes people have to learn their stage, because every rest in life, neither takes you fitter nor clever and the columns that comes, with it, neither awake you nor mistake you; just remember, it is your voice, neither to succumb system or mystery…

Sometimes people have to burn their rage, because every request in life, either shakes you quitter or inspector and the bottoms that comes, with it, either snake you or partake you; just remember, it is your choice, either to dumb symptom or contradictory…

Sometimes people have to earn their engage, because every best in life, neither aches you sitter nor getter and the volumes that comes, with it, neither fake you nor betake you; just remember, it is your rejoice, neither to sum wisdom or history…

Stay prayed up…

Quote for Today

Day 67

Body

We all have some type of blemish, rather it is a cut, a scar, a burn, a pimple, a blackhead, a ingrown hair, a cyst, even a permanent which is a birthmark...

We fall behalf come hype of replenish, gather admit this is a gut, a char, a stern, a dimple, a whitehead, a prone tear, a wrist, and even the determinant above a girth arc...

The point is the formation of the body is made to be punctured or damaged...

The moral is the confirmation of the embody is persuade to be structured or managed...

Stay prayed up...

Quote for Today

Day 68

Obstacles

Observe, because sometimes the attitude could lead endless sadly…

With this obstacle, have no fear, beware, and dare to represent it, following the rules so badly…

Obey, because sometimes the actions causes lost enemies snappy…

With this obstacle, do not stare, prepare, and make clear, to present wit, no sorrowing the clues so gladly…

Obstruct, because sometimes the attention creates less energy scrappy…

With this obstacle, flare, impair, but instead declare to prevent conflict, your shallowing do not confuse avoid the madly…

The point is that obstacle could be used as lessons, something you have done, or something that you do, example, this is my obstacle of doing my quotes…

The moral is that obstacle could be amused as blessings, nothing but to have fun, nothing only pay your dues, sample, wish on my obstacle of pursuing my notes…

Stay prayed up…

Quote for Today

Day 69

Looks

Some people have a hype, which is their own type of beauty…

Some people are classy, which how dare to be flashy, and a cutie…

Some people are nasty, which to be appeared as trashy, their main duties…

Some people are quiet, which indicates their silence, either perky or moody…

Some people are loud, which to be unbothered and proud, unknown or known snooty…

Stay prayed up…

Quote for Today

Day 70

Darkness

Some people are bright, which could be their fight, leery, and or beast...

Some people are chill, which could be hidden real, but too much is released...

Some people are ignorant, which their stance is belligerent, and no increase...

Some people are serious, which they are not curious, neutral no more but at least...

Stay prayed up...

Quote for Today

Day 71

The Card Game

Sometimes when people deal, it could indicate what is being dealt, a shade, but in reality it should be a spade...

Sometimes when people deal, it could indicate their scars and welp, a rub, but the mentality it would be a club...

Sometimes when people deal, it could indicate what was felt, a nine, but in nationality it could be a diamond...

Sometimes when people deal, it could indicate a kind of yelp, a part, but in actuality it would be a heart...

Stay prayed up...

Quote for Today

Day 72

Clueless

Sometimes the existence, "the person," could be a sign of discipline, indicating their unknown philosophy...

Sometimes the persistence, "the assertion," could be a incline, perpetrating their own epistemology...

Sometimes the resistance, "the version," could be a confine, vindicating their shown axiology...

Sometimes the insistence, "the diversion," could be a combine, instigating their unblown sociology...

Stay prayed up...

Quote for Today

Day 73

Stay in Your Lane

Sometimes when people mind other people's business, their mission is unethical to manage, which could influence your task and their own type of social responsibility…

Sometimes when people find other people's slickness, their vision is hypothetical damage, which could discontinuance your dask and their condone hype of emotional ability…

Sometimes when people kind other people's strictness, their collusion is skeptical to adage, which could confluence your slack and their postpone snipe of notional susceptibility…

Stay prayed up…

Quote for Today

Day 74

The Rumble

Sometimes the people who you think would be there no matter what, through ups and downs, are the ones who let you down…

Sometimes the people who you sink could be there no matter what, through lumps and frowns, are the ones set you around…

Stay prayed up…

Quote for Today

Day 75

The Path

Guidance is first towards being a leader...

Violence is worst towards being a beater...

Silence is better than unnecessary drama...

Compliance is better than unnecessary trauma...

The point is whether you indulge in drama or trauma, just be careful, it's something called karma...

The moral is whether you begrudge in leader or beater, just be prayful, it's something called speaker...

Stay prayed up...

Quote for Today

Day 76

School

Sometimes when it comes to learning, people may use their English improperly, but their skills are scientific, which could sum up their own creativity...

Sometimes when it comes to turning, people may use their distinguish properly, but their fulfills are hieroglyphic, which could numb up their shown selectivity...

Sometimes when it comes to concerning, people may use their extinguish scholarly, but their instills are prolific, which should um up their grown progressivity...

Sometimes when it comes to returning, people may use their relinquish property, but their thrills are terrific, which should glum up their flown activity...

Stay prayed up...

Quote for Today

Day 77

Workplace

When it comes to work, some people give their all, and some people don't, which could make the job harder or easy…

When it comes to smirk, some people relive their fall, and some people won't, which could take the prob tarter or queasy…

When it comes to berserk, some people live their call, and some people don't, which could fake the sob farther or peasy…

When it comes to lurk, some people forgive their stall, and some people won't, which would awake the throb smarter or greasy…

Stay prayed up…

Quote for Today

Day 78

Proven

Sometimes when words are spoken, you hear and listen, pay close attention, remember don't just let people talk, let them act...

Sometimes when words are broken, you disappear and ambition, away those mention, remember don't let them just say, let them show...

Sometimes when words are awoken, you clear and glisten, pray diagnose comprehension, remember don't let them promise, let them prove...

The main point of it all...

Don't talk, act...

Don't say, show...

Don't promise, prove...

Stay prayed up...

Quote for Today

Day 79

Drugs

Their are illegal drugs, which some people sell, and others may use, do not corrupt your doings, remember this could lead in the wrong place...

Their are diesel thugs, which some dwell, and others play abuse, do not interrupt your brewings, remember this would bleed in the strong trace...

Their are prescription drugs, which some people need, and others say refuse, do not disrupt your foolings, remember this could head in the long race...

Their are subscription plugs, which some people proceed and others pray disabuse, do not erupt your renewings, remember this would indeed in the along pace...

Stay prayed up...

Quote for Today

Day 80

Plants

Sometimes people plant and grow their seed, and some people roll and smoke their weed, which could be earthly from the ground...

Sometimes people can't and show their speed, and some people console and choke their breed, which could be adversely from the underground...

Sometimes people grant and flow their greed, and some people control and provoke their need, which could be absurdly from the compound...

The point is, be alert, aware, and chant of what you do...

The moral is, overt, beware, and plant of what you grew...

Stay prayed up...

Quote for Today

Day 81

Sleeping Heavy

Sometimes when people sleep, some people make noise, some people are quiet, and some people may dream...

Sometimes when people peep, some people fake enjoys, some people stay silent, and some people stay scheme...

Sometimes when people creep, some people take poise, some people bizarre violent, and some people display extreme...

Sometimes when people deep, some people shake destroys, some people far complaint, and some people say scream...

Sometimes when people keep, some people partake annoys, some people scar suppliant, and some people pray redeem...

Stay prayed up...

Quote for Today

Day 82

The Interruption

Sometimes people will pray on your downfall, while others will give you praise, watch and notice who they be...

Sometimes people still say on your drown call, defile others will give you raise, botch and focus knew they degree...

Sometimes people until away on your clown appall, versatile others will give you phrase, panache and bogus through they agree...

Sometimes people skill okay on your crown install, file others will give you phase, topnotch and bonus clue they free...

Stay prayed up...

Quote for Today

Day 83

Loud and Clear

When people speak, learn what they are speaking, not spoken, listen to the lyrics, understanding if it is denied or purified…

When people write, concern what they are writing, not wroten, vision to the metempirics, undemanding if it is satisfied or qualified…

The point is when spoken or wroten is used, it indicates past tense, so let it make suspense…

The moral is when speaking or writing is enthused, it evaluates last condense, so let it make sense…

Stay prayed up…

Quote for Today

Day 84

The Quiet Storm

When people say skies are the limit, it could mean it will rain, it could mean it could storm, or it could mean it will be sunny…

When people pay ties are the digit, it could deem it will gain, it could deem it could norm, or it could deem it will be funny…

When people decay dies the explicit, it could lean it will obtain, it could lean it could reform, or it could lean it will be runny…

When people pray wise the spirit, it could gene it will remain, it could gene it could form, or it could gene it will be honey…

Stay prayed up…

Quote for Today

Day 85

Two Sides

Some people like the heat, because it gets them hot, it gets them angry, which is why they give disappointment...

Some people like the cool, because it gets them pot, it gets them cranky, which is why they give people enjoyment...

Some people like the backseat, because it gets them forgot, it gets them stinky, which is imply they give people contentment...

Some people like it fool, because it gets them a lot, it get them gangly, which is imply they give people appointment...

The point is, if people are angry, cranky, stinky, or gangly, they could be at their boiling point, always stay away...

The moral is, if people are hot, pot, forgot, or a lot, they should be at their recoiling joint, always pray yay...

Stay prayed up...

Quote for Today

Day 86

Break Through

Some people have been through more than you can expect...

Some people have been through sore than you can protect...

Some people have been through core than you can detect...

Some people have been through ignore than you can neglect...

Some people have been through explore than you can elect...

Some people have been through score than you can respect...

Stay prayed up...

Quote for Today

Day 87

Born or Torn

Some people are born talkers, some people are born walkers, which does not make them different, that is how they were made...

Some people are torn stalkers, some people are torn brawlers, which does not take them magnificent, that is how they were trade...

The point is, if a person was born a talker or stalker, acknowledge they are able to do so...

The moral is, if a person was torn a stalker or brawler, blockage they are unstable to do no...

Stay prayed up...

Quote for Today

Day 88

Shake It Off

Sometimes when people's mind start rattling, it could relate to common sense or something dense…

Sometimes when people's grind apart battling, it could mediate to uncommon defense or nothing intense…

The point is, start and apart ends with "art," which you get to paint the picture and sculpture creativity…

The moral common and uncommon ends with "on," switch to acquaint literature and puncture progressivity…

Stay prayed up…

Quote for Today

Day 89

Friends

Sometimes people are cocky with their friends, which could lead to distraction…

Sometimes people are rocky with their friends, which would plead to reaction…

Sometimes people are jockey with their friends, which should head to satisfaction…

The point is, know who your real friends are they come in a small package…

The moral is, grow who your deal friends star they come in a tall babbage…

Stay prayed up…

Quote for Today

Day 90

No Matter What

No matter what the circumstances may be, keep a smile and make it your deliverance…

No matter what the enhances may see, deep a denial and make it your considerance…

Continue your journey even if there's a dip…

Venue your sterny even if tears a rip…

Stay prayed up…

Quote for Today

Day 91

Understand

When you are happy, feel good, and keep your spirits high...

When you are snappy, feel stood, and reaping your demerits sigh...

When you are clappy, feel understood, and peeping your coherents fly...

The point is good, stood, and understood is the main baseline...

The moral is high, sigh, and fly is the pain brakeline...

Stay prayed up...

Quote for Today

Day 92

The Near-sighted

Be mindful what type of people you be around…

Be kindful on what hype of people you see clown…

Be grindful on what skype of people you plea pound…

Sometimes people will put on a show, fake…

Sometimes people will put on a glow, snake…

Sometimes people will put on a grow, take…

Stay prayed up…

Quote for Today

Day 93

Lesson

Sometimes when people make statements, it could indicate being funny, straight up, or their own fought...

Sometimes when people take debatements, it would humiliate being ugly, made up, or their own thoughts...

The point is, no matter the statement or debatement, remember you could be better than that...

The moral is, no matter the fought or thought, remember you should be better than combat...

Stay prayed up...

Quote for Today

Day 94

Prepared

Always be prepared for the good or worst, peep it, oh it is happening...

Always be aware for the understood or reversed, keep it, no it is saddening...

Always be care for the hood or cursed, reap it, so it is baddening...

Stay prayed up...

Quote for Today

Day 95

The Memorize

Remember, when things are done it could be a blessing, taking care of importance matters…

Remember, when strings far fun it is a testing, making fair of accordance flatters…

Remember, when flings are won it could be a stressing, taking dare of performance batters…

Remember, when brings are run it could be a addressing, making pair of discordance shatters…

Stay prayed up…

Quote for Today

Day 96

The Move

Stay away from people who cool with people who not cool with you, best to believe they play both sides…

Pray away from people who fool with people who plot fool with you, best to receive they say both divides…

Lay away from people who bool with people who spot bool with you, best to relieve they pay both provides…

May away from people who drool with people who slot drool with you, best to perceive they slay both rides…

Stay prayed up…

Quote for Today

Day 97

Piano

Some people take people with a great heart, but with a strong mind, unpredictable…

Some people make people with a straight start, but with a wrong kind, irresistible…

Some people take people with a relate part, but with a belong sign, replaceable…

Some people make people with a debate chart, but with a long align, despicable…

Some people take people with a slate smart, but with a song combined, acceptable…

Some people with a negate subpart, but with a prolong entwined, correctable…

Stay prayed up…

Quote for Today

Day 98

The Cookbook

Sometimes when people cook, some people cook fast, some people cook slow, which could indicate how their stirring is done...

Sometimes when people hook, some people hook bash, some people hook so, which could indicate how their preparing is run...

Sometimes when people book know, some people book smash, some book row, which could indicate their airing is ton...

Sometimes when people crook low, some people crook last, some people crook no, which could indicate how their baring is spun...

Stay prayed up...

Quote for Today

Day 99

The Show-case

Sometimes when people are defensive, it could indicate their past story, or just how they are, which sometimes is the reflection of self...

Sometimes when people are sensitive, it could initiate their last glory, or just wow they star, which sometimes is the perfection of thyself...

Sometimes when people are offensive, it could integrate their blast prehistory, or just bow their ajar, which sometimes is the detection of oneself...

Sometimes when people are ostensive, it could vibrate their cast inventory, or just pow their afar, which sometimes is the intellection of nonself...

Stay prayed up...

Quote for My Way

Day 100

Antonia's Mentality and Reality

I will start by saying, my favorite subject is English, and I admire reading and writing...

I still chart by saying, my favorite reject is distinguish, and I hire succeeding and citing...

I have written stories, music, quotes, and did much more, something I will make time for...

I have spittin' glories, cubic, notes, and hid touch score, nothing I pill take rhyme sore...

Back in time, I had stacks of books of strategy indicating my type of work I do...

Track in mind, I had packs of hooks of audacity indicating my hype of twerk I knew...

Dancing is another side that I represent, and serve as my well-being, true story...

Advancing is farther pride that I present, and deserve as my tell bringing, new glories...

One point, I took a long wait, and stopped my processing, and threw away all my ideals...

None disappoint, I shook a belong straight, and popped my accessing, and knew stay all my forreals…

In school, in college, I put in so much effort and was eager to learn, headed to my number 1 class…

Win cool, win knowledge, I put in grow touch desert and was meager to earn to my number fun pass…

Neglecting, when I threw out all my buildings, and original pages, I thought it was all over…

Respecting, when I withdrew about all my shielding's, and decisional stages, I fought it cause all trover…

The date when I began my goal again, I declared to keep going, in the right direction…

The state when I ran my soul twin, I starred to peep growing, in the light selection…

I made dope slides, I made a known picture of who I am, just with paper and pen…

I fade nope tides, I fade a grown literature of who I ma'am bless labor and Amen…

My syllables and punctuation, use to be underlined by the teacher, always making corrections…

Why livable and occupation, profuse to thee designed by the Reacher, hallways taking perfection…

When it came to my citations, I tried the repeated until I got it, and felt accomplished...

When it fame to my creation, I cried the defeated dwell I knot it, and spelt astonished...

Once I seen my red light, and then green tight, I guess I was undecided, and I said it can't be...

Bunce I lean my dead fright, and then routine sight, I mess I was provided, and I read plant me...

Recovering and picking up where I left off, I endorsed my mentality that my notes are the legit...

Discovering and sticking up where I deft aloft, I enforced my reality that my quotes are the shit...

I darted the ink and marched back into my gift, never giving up, just printing on the dotted lines...

I restarted the rethink and arched track into my width, clever living sup, success squinting on the spotted resigns...

Many mistakes and some tutoring, I scored and maintained a grade of high...

Many fakes and some rumoring, I adored and contained a invade of a sigh...

Brainstorming and wondering about my documentation of what I study, my spoken words of what I wrote...

Forming and numbering route my accusation of what I buddy, my token heards of what I promote...

Now that I'm serious, and on my mission to do what I like to do best, I'm content and will not lose...

Wow that I'm curious, and on my submission to pursue what I like to pursue request, I'm indent and fulfill a lot renew...

I went out to the store to buy all supplies, to get back on my journey, surrendering to get my book completed...

I sent shout to the adore to tie all implies, to fit that on my worthy, gendering to fit my overlook greeted...

Unsure about the punctuations, explanation points, and sometimes periods, I practiced and then knew where they belonged, a slight fight...

Mature route formations, examination joints, and sometimes serious, I exactness and then grew swear they stronged, polite right...

My mind lead, while my hand said, Antonia, you have the talent, and do not let it go unnoticed, you got this...

My grind plead, while my stand fled, claustrophobia you have the balance, stand do not regret it no unfocused, you hot sis...

Now that I have built up back my pages, and tradition to my notes of being a dedicated writer of my own, okay slayed...

Pow that I have skilled jack up my engages, and edition to my quotes, being an educated rider above my shown, say prayed...

Sometimes I started off with drafts, sometimes I drifted, but at the end of the day, my pen stayed lifted, oh of course...

Sometimes I charted soft with graphs, sometimes I shifted, but at the recommend of the way, my sin prayed gifted, so of endorse...

Yes, it was difficult and hard to make it work, no it was not easy to put it together, but I strived for better and greatness...

Bless, it was mythical and disregarded to make it rework, so it was a lot peasy to put it wherever, but I survived for pleasure and faithfulness...

My faults and taughts, my ups and downs, my loss, my gain, I finally made it to the finish line, of one of my projects...

Shy defaults and thoughts, my disrupts and frowns, my frost, my pain, I finally made it to the extinguish time, of one of my objects...

Never giving up, never quitting, I will always use what I got (writing), to get what I want my (book), and it will be continued...

Forever living up, forever ripping, I will always amuse what I plot (typing) to get what I stunt (look), and it still be menued...

Visit:www.antoniaquotes@reality.com/followed by...

Quizit:www.antonianotes@mentality.com/modeledby...

I win. The end.

Stay prayed up.